General
MATHEMATICS

The Scottish Certificate of Education Examination Papers
are reprinted by special permission of
THE SCOTTISH QUALIFICATIONS AUTHORITY

Note: The answers to the questions do not emanate from the Authority.

ISBN 0 7169 9302 3
© *Robert Gibson & Sons, Glasgow, Ltd., 1999*

ROBERT GIBSON · Publisher
17 Fitzroy Place, Glasgow, G3 7SF.

SCOTTISH CERTIFICATE OF EDUCATION

MATHEMATICS

Standard Grade — GENERAL LEVEL

Time: 1 hour 30 minutes

INSTRUCTIONS TO CANDIDATES

1. Answer as many questions as you can.

2. Write your working and answers in the spaces provided. Additional space is provided at the end of the question-answer book for use if required. If you use this space, write clearly the number of the question involved.

3. Full credit will be given only where the solution contains appropriate working.

4. Before leaving the examination room you must give this book to the Invigilator. If you do not you may lose all the marks for this paper.

FORMULAE LIST

General Papers

Circumference of a circle: $C = \pi d$

Area of circle: $A = \pi r^2$

Curved surface area of a cylinder: $A = 2\pi rh$

Volume of a cylinder: $V = \pi r^2 h$

Volume of a triangular prism: $V = Ah$

Theorem of Pythagoras:

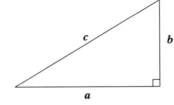

$$a^2 + b^2 = c^2$$

Trigonometric ratios
in a right angled
triangle:

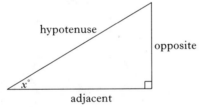

$$\tan x° = \frac{\text{opposite}}{\text{adjacent}}$$

$$\sin x° = \frac{\text{opposite}}{\text{hypotenuse}}$$

$$\cos x° = \frac{\text{adjacent}}{\text{hypotenuse}}$$

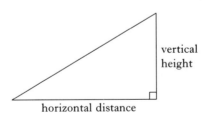

$$\text{Gradient} = \frac{\text{vertical height}}{\text{horizontal distance}}$$

SCOTTISH
CERTIFICATE OF
EDUCATION
1993

TUESDAY, 11 MAY
11.50 AM – 12.20 PM

MATHEMATICS
STANDARD GRADE
General Level

Marks | KU | RA

1. Two garages are selling the same model of car for the same price.

   One garage asks for a £500 deposit and 12 equal payments of £750.

   The other garage asks for a £1100 deposit and 24 equal payments.

   How much should each payment be?

   (4)

2. Write 3^5 as a whole number.

   (2)

3. The diagram shows a Magic Triangle.

   It is "magic" because the total of the numbers along each of the three sides is the same.

   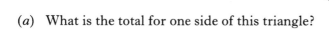

   (a) What is the total for one side of this triangle?

   (1)

   (b) Use the numbers −2, −1, 1 and 2 to complete the magic triangle below, where the total for each side is 2.

   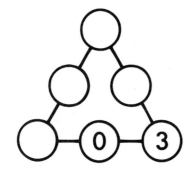

   (3)

Marks KU RA

4. Mallaig and Lochboisdale are two small ports in the Northwest of Scotland.

The scale drawing shows the positions of Mallaig and Lochboisdale, which are 95 kilometres apart.

N

N

Lochboisdale

Mallaig

(a) Write down the scale of the drawing.

(2)

(b) A third port, Castlebay, is on a bearing of 210° from Lochboisdale and is due West of Mallaig.

Complete the scale drawing above to show the position of Castlebay. (3)

(c) Use the scale drawing to find the distance in kilometres between Castlebay and Lochboisdale.

(2)

5. Mr and Mrs Politi want to buy a house valued at £87 500. They need a loan of £84 000.

The Homesure Building Society lends up to 95% of the value of a house.

Will Mr and Mrs Politi be able to borrow the money they need from the Homesure Building Society?

Give a reason for your answer.

(3)

Marks KU RA

6. Allanton Youth Opera has a logo using the initials A, Y and O.

Part of the logo is shown below.

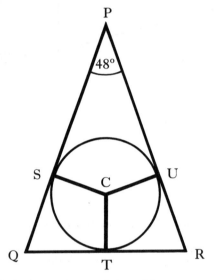

Triangle PQR is isosceles and its sides are tangents to the circle at S, T and U.

C is the centre of the circle.

The angle at P is 48°.

(*a*) Calculate the size of the angle at R.

(1)

(*b*) Explain why the angles at U are right angles.

(1)

(*c*) Calculate the size of angle TCU.

(1)

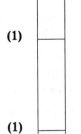

6

7. The graph shows the monthly attendances at a water leisure centre from January 1990 to January 1993.

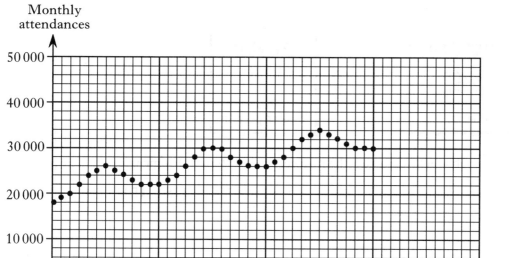

(a) Describe the **overall** trend of the graph.

(1)

(b) Describe what happened to the attendances from January 1992 to January 1993.

(2)

(c) Estimate the attendance in July 1993.

(2)

8. Chris needs to use a ladder to put up a television aerial on the wall of the house.

The ladder is 5 metres long and has to reach 4·8 metres up the wall.

For safety, the angle between the ladder and the ground should be between 71° and 76°.

The ground is horizontal.

Can Chris use this ladder safely?

You must give a reason for your answer.

(5)

9. Mr and Mrs Tang are visiting Scotland and decide to hire a car for a week.

The car hire company has two different schemes for hiring a car, the Freedom and the Rover.

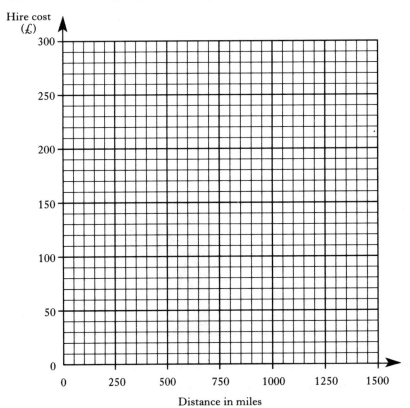

FREEDOM
£205
per week
All inclusive

ROVER
£145
per week
PLUS
6 pence per mile

(a) Complete the table below to show the hire costs for different distances.

Number of miles	0	250	500	750	1000	1250	1500
"FREEDOM": cost in £							
"ROVER": cost in £							

(3)

(b) (i) On the grid opposite, draw a graph to show the hire costs using the Freedom scheme. **(1)**

   (ii) On the same grid, draw a graph showing the Rover hire costs. **(1)**

(c) Mr and Mrs Tang plan to drive about 200 miles every day.

Which scheme would be better for them?

Give a reason.

(2)

Marks KU RA

Marks | KU | RA

10. David, Malcolm and Kate all collect badges.

David has twice as many badges as Kate.

Malcolm has 12 badges less than Kate.

Kate has x badges.

(a) Write down, in terms of x,

    (i) how many badges David has,

    (ii) how many badges Malcolm has.

    (2)

(b) If David, Malcolm and Kate have 80 badges altogether, write down an equation and solve it to find x.

    (4)

11. Mrs Carter went to a jumble sale where she bought a box of picture bricks for her daughter.

The bricks are cubes of side 5 centimetres and they completely fill the box, which is a larger cube of side 20 centimetres.

(a) How many bricks are there?

    (2)

(b) The pictures on the bricks are worn and dirty so Mrs Carter wants to cover the sides of all the bricks with stick-on plastic.

The plastic comes in a roll which is 30 centimetres wide.

What length of plastic does Mrs Carter need?

    (3)

12. (*a*) Complete the table below for $y = 2x + 1$.

x	-4	0	4
y			

(2)

(*b*) Using the table in part (*a*), draw the graph of the line $y = 2x + 1$ on the grid.

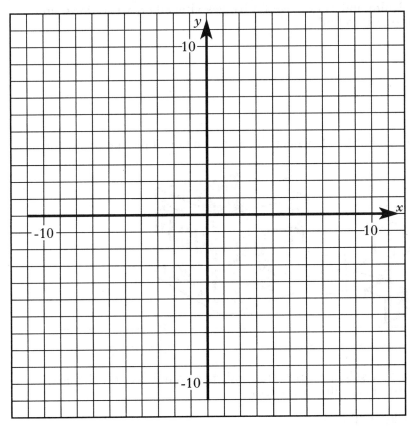

(2)

(*c*) What is the gradient of this line?

(1)

Marks | KU | RA

13. Mike and Alan are doing an experiment to show that the weight of a steel bar, W grams, varies directly with its length, L centimetres.

The table below shows their results.

LENGTH OF BAR (L CENTIMETRES)	3·2	4·8	10	16	18·4	22
WEIGHT OF BAR (W GRAMS)	40	60	125	200	230	275

Explain how these results can be used to find out if the weight of the bar varies directly with its length.

(3)

14. A satellite travels in a circular orbit round the earth once every $2\frac{1}{2}$ hours.

The satellite is 2900 kilometres above the earth's surface.

The earth has a radius of 6400 kilometres.

(a) What is the radius of the orbit of the satellite?

(1)

(b) Calculate the speed of the satellite.

(4)

11

Marks KU RA

15. A banner is to be edged all round with gold braid.

The banner is in the shape of a rectangle with an isosceles triangle below it, as shown in the diagram.

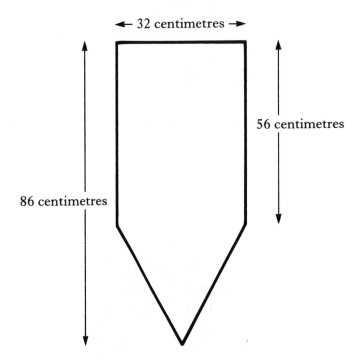

Calculate the total length of gold braid needed.

(5)

16. After a test, a teacher worked out the average mark for her class of 10 pupils. It was 81%.

One of the pupils scored only 27%, which was much less than any of the other marks.

The teacher decided to work out a new average, leaving out the lowest mark.

What was the new average?

(3)

17. Mr Jones is fixing a plastic gutter along the top of his garage wall.

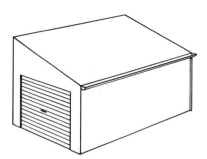

The cross-section of the gutter is a semi-circle.

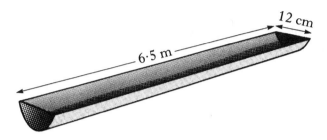

The diameter of the semi-circle is 12 centimetres.

The length of the gutter is 6·5 metres.

(*a*) How many litres of water will this gutter hold when full?

(5)

(*b*) The gutter must be supported 10 centimetres from each end and at equal intervals along its length. The supports must not be more than a metre apart.

Calculate the smallest number of supports needed and how far apart they should be placed. (Ignore the width of the support.)

(4)

[END OF QUESTION PAPER]

Marks | KU | RA

1. Iain has bought video equipment costing £1850 and wants to insure it.

   The insurance company charges £1·16 for every £100 of goods to be insured.

   What will it cost Iain to insure his video equipment?

   (3)

2. The graph shows some information about two boys, Alexander and Darren.

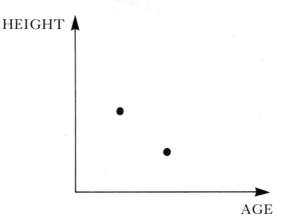

HEIGHT

AGE

   Alexander is older than Darren.

   (a) Label the dots on the graph with the names of the two boys. **(1)**

   (b) What else does the graph tell you about the boys?

   (2)

   (c) Claire is the same age as Darren and is taller than both boys.

   Show this information by marking a dot on the graph above. **(2)**

Marks KU RA

3. The diagram below shows a triangular flag which is 28 centimetres across and 46 centimetres long.

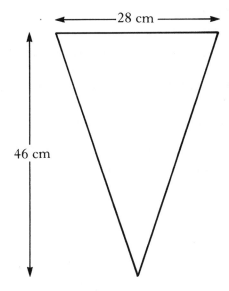

Calculate the area of the flag.

(3)

Marks KU | RA

4. Mr and Mrs Campbell's children have had their photographs taken at school.

The photographs are available in the following packs.

PACK A costs £8·00
PACK B costs £6·50
PACK C costs £5·50

Mr and Mrs Campbell want to buy 3 packs of photographs but decide to spend not more than £20 in total.

One way they could do this is to buy 1 of pack B and 2 of pack C which would cost a total of £17·50.

This is shown in the first row of the table below.

Number of Pack A	Number of Pack B	Number of Pack C
	1	2

(a) Fill in the rest of the table to show all the different ways Mr and Mrs Campbell could buy 3 packs of photographs of their children. **(3)**

(b) They choose the way that gives them the largest number of photographs, but they still spend not more than £20 in total.

PACK A contains 1 large, 2 medium and 4 small photographs.
PACK B contains 1 large and 2 medium photographs.
PACK C contains 2 medium and 2 small photographs.

Which packs do they buy and how many photographs is this in total?

You must show all your working.

(3)

Marks | KU | RA

5. The pie chart shows how an agricultural company spent £86 000 000 in one year on machinery, spares and repairs.

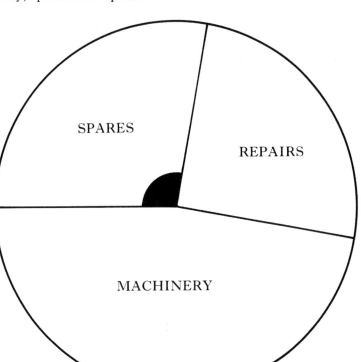

(*a*) Measure the size of the shaded angle.

(1)

(*b*) Calculate the amount of money spent on spares, giving your answer to the nearest million pounds.

(3)

Marks | KU | RA

6. Two estate agents charge different amounts for selling a house.

<table>
<tr><td>

TIMSON AND CO

CHARGES:

$1\frac{1}{2}$% OF THE HOUSE VALUE

</td><td>

WILSON AND LYLE

CHARGES:

2% OF THE HOUSE VALUE UP TO £30 000

PLUS

1% OF THE HOUSE VALUE ABOVE £30 000

</td></tr>
</table>

Mr and Mrs Bernstein want to sell their house which has a value of £70 000.

Which estate agent should they use?

You must show all your working.

(5)

7. The diagram below shows the positions of three towns, Belford, Hoylake and Liston.

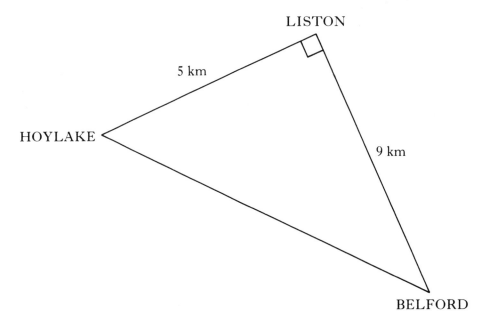

Calculate the distance from Hoylake to Belford.

Give your answer correct to 1 decimal place.

(3)

8.

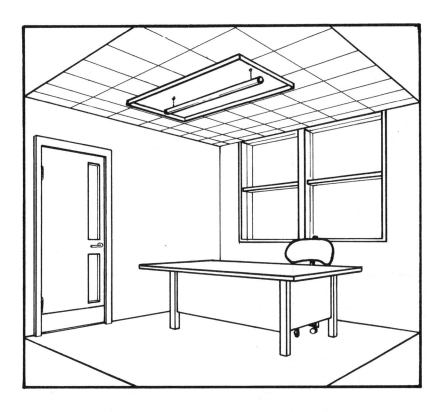

The amount of light needed in an office depends on its room index, R.

$$R = \frac{LW}{H(L + W)}$$

where   L metres is the length of the office,

W metres is the width of the office,

H metres is the height of the light above the desk.

Calculate the room index for an office 5·5 metres long and 4·2 metres wide, with the light 1·3 metres above the desk.

(3)

9. (*a*) On the coordinate diagram below, plot the points

$$(-7, 0), \quad (-2, -8) \quad \text{and} \quad (6, -3).$$

(2)

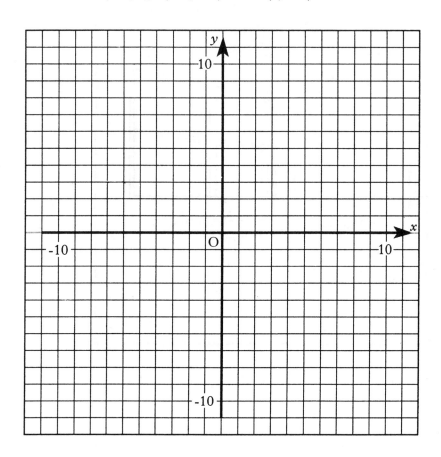

(*b*) The three points above are three corners of a square.

On the same diagram, plot the point which is the fourth corner of the square.

(1)

Marks | KU | RA

10. A superstore has three kinds of paint.

£3·99   £4·99   £6·49

(a) Using the information shown above, explain why Coverite appears to give the best value for money.

(2)

(b) On the backs of the tins there is more information.

Using this additional information, decide which paint is the best value for money.

You must show all your working.

(3)

11. The diagram shows a ramp connecting two levels in a shopping centre.

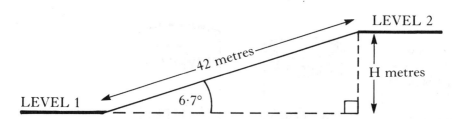

The ramp is 42 metres long, and slopes at an angle of 6·7°, as shown in the diagram.

Calculate the difference in height, H metres, between the two levels.

(4)

12. Three friends set off on an 820 kilometre journey.

They travel at an average speed of 80 kilometres per hour.

How long will the journey take?

Give your answer in hours and minutes.

(3)

Marks | KU | RA

13. Water is stored in a tank.

When the water level falls to a certain depth, the tank is automatically refilled.

The graph below shows the depth of water in the tank during a period of 24 hours.

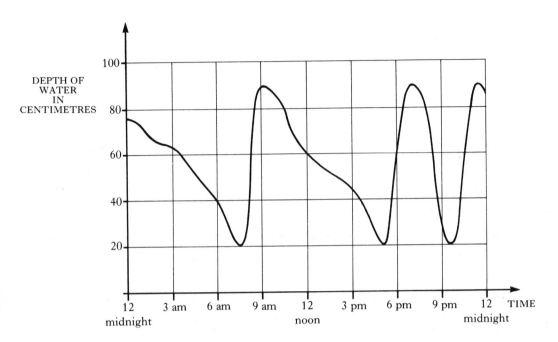

(*a*) How many times was the tank refilled during the 24 hours?

(1)

(*b*) What is the depth of the water when the tank has just been refilled?

(1)

(*c*) The water tank is in the shape of a cuboid of length 1·5 metres and breadth 1·2 metres.

How many litres of water are in the tank when it has just been refilled?

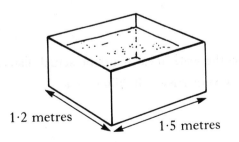

1·2 metres   1·5 metres

(3)

Marks | KU | RA

14. Solve the inequality

$$2(x + 3) < 18.$$

(3)

15. The drawing shows part of a map.
The two dots represent hilltops.

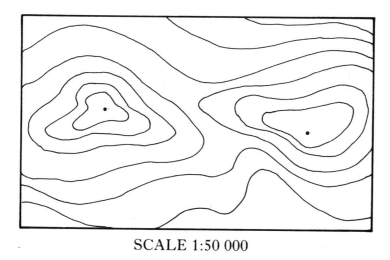

SCALE 1:50 000

(*a*) Measure the distance between the dots on the map.

(1)

(*b*) Use the scale to calculate the actual distance between the hilltops.
Give your answer in kilometres.

(3)

Marks | KU | RA

16. A running track is being marked out as shown below.

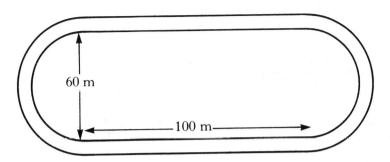

The straight part of the track is 100 metres long and the width across the inside of the track is 60 metres. The ends of the track are semi-circular.

(*a*) Calculate the perimeter of the inside of the track.

(3)

(*b*) The completed track has 4 lanes as shown below.

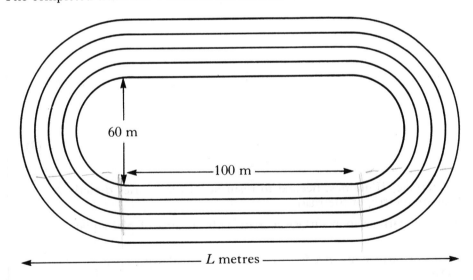

The lines marking the lanes are 1 metre apart.

Calculate the overall length, *L* metres, of the track.

(3)

17. A new swimming pool is 30 metres long and 12 metres wide.

The depth of the pool at the shallow end is to be 1 metre.

It is proposed that the depth at the deep end is 2·5 metres.

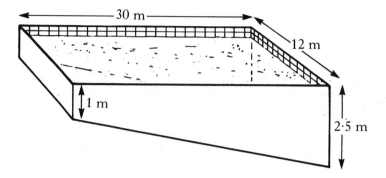

Regulations state that the slope of the bottom of the pool must be less than 0·07.

The slope can be calculated using the rule

$$\text{slope} = \frac{\text{change in depth of pool, in metres}}{\text{length of pool, in metres}}$$

Will the new pool satisfy the regulations?

You must give a reason for your answer.

(3)

18. The quantity of tarmac, W tonnes, needed to resurface a road varies directly as the area, A square metres, of the road.

It takes 54 tonnes of tarmac to resurface a road with an area of 600 square metres.

How many tonnes of tarmac are needed to resurface a road with an area of 1100 square metres?

(4)

Marks | KU | RA

19. A company makes rectangular cards of different sizes. The cards are coded according to their size.

R1 is 1 centimetre by 2 centimetres

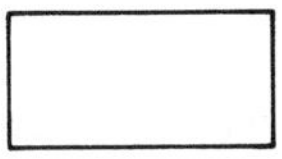

R2 is 2 centimetres by 3 centimetres

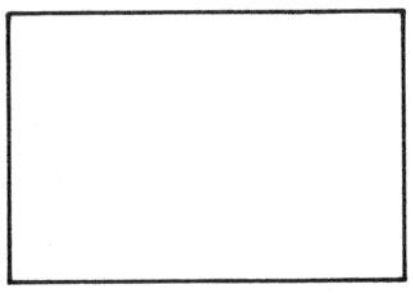

R3 is 3 centimetres by 4 centimetres

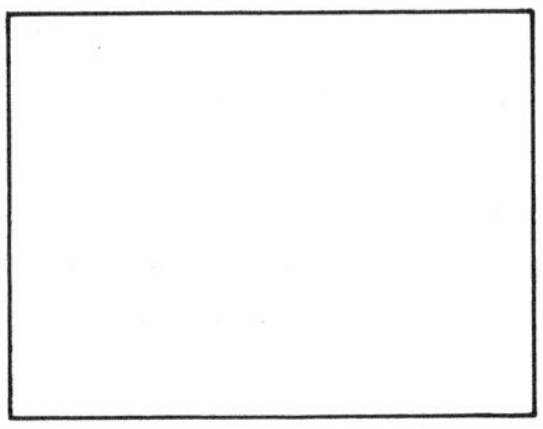

and so on.

(*a*) Write down the size of the next card, R4.

(1)

(*b*) How many R4 pieces of card can be cut from an R10 piece of card?
You must explain your answer.

(4)

[END OF QUESTION PAPER]

SCOTTISH
CERTIFICATE OF
EDUCATION
1995

FRIDAY, 5 MAY
10.50 AM – 12.20 PM

MATHEMATICS
STANDARD GRADE
General Level

Marks | KU | RA

1. Salvatore is going back to Italy to visit his parents.

   He wants to exchange £160 into Lire.

Country	Rate per £
Austria	16·70 Schillings
France	8·15 Francs
Greece	365·00 Drachmas
Italy	2390·00 Lire
Spain	196·58 Pesetas

   How many Lire will he get? **(2)**

2. The table shows the average winter temperatures in four cities.

	London	New York	Rome	Moscow
Average winter temperature	3 °C	–2 °C	6 °C	–8 °C

   (a) What is the difference between the average winter temperatures in London and Moscow? **(2)**

   (b) One winter's day, the temperature in New York was 7 degrees below average.

   What was the temperature that day? **(1)**

3. The workers in a factory were voting on a proposed pay offer.

   $\frac{5}{8}$ of the 368 workers voted to accept the offer.

   How many workers was this? **(2)**

Marks | KU | RA

4. Anne is trying to guess Martin's phone number. She knows it has four figures.

Martin tells Anne that the first three figures are all the same and that the sum of all four figures is 15.

(a) Write down all the possible four-figure numbers that fit the description of Martin's phone number.

(3)

(b) Martin now tells Anne that the last figure is a prime number.

Write down Martin's phone number.

(1)

5. The table below appeared in a newspaper and shows when street lights should come on and go off.

Lighting-up Times			
London	4.43 pm	to	7.44 am
Bristol	4.52 pm	to	7.53 am
Birmingham	4.46 pm	to	7.54 am
Manchester.....................	4.43 pm	to	8.00 am
Newcastle......................	4.35 pm	to	8.03 am
Glasgow	4.41 pm	to	8.17 am
Belfast	4.54 pm	to	8.18 am

(a) How long, in hours and minutes, were the street lights on in Glasgow?

(2)

(b) Was the time of year summer or winter?
You must give a reason for your answer.

(2)

6. A large box is filled with packets of rice.

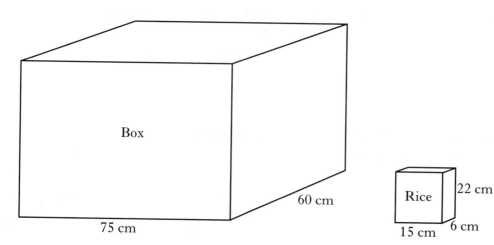

Each packet measures 15 centimetres by 6 centimetres by 22 centimetres and the packets are stacked upright in the box.

(*a*) How many packets fit exactly into the base of the box?

(2)

(*b*) When full, the box contains 150 packets.
What is the height of the box?

(3)

(*c*) How many boxes could be stacked on top of each other in a space which is 5 metres high?
Show all your working.

(3)

Marks	KU	RA

Marks | KU | RA

7. This advertisement appeared in a newspaper.

STRATHCLYDE THEATRE

	ADULT	CHILD
Balcony	£12	£8
Front Stalls	£10	£6
Back Stalls	£8	£5

Phone for details of
Special Prices for Mid-week Show

A school telephoned for details of the special prices for the mid-week show. Tickets for seats in the back stalls were bought for 20 pupils and 2 teachers. The tickets cost a total of £60.

(a) How much did the school save?

(3)

(b) The teachers paid £5 each for their tickets.
How much did each pupil's ticket cost?

(3)

Marks | KU | RA

8. The diagram shows an island drawn to a scale of 1 centimetre to 20 kilometres.

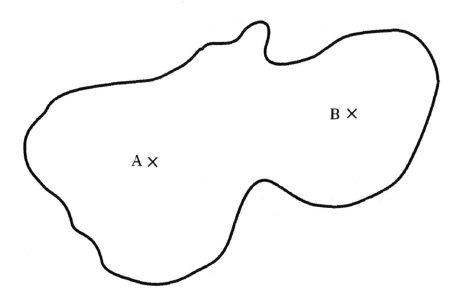

Scale: 1 cm to 20 km

The island has 2 radio transmitters.

The transmitter at A has a range of 80 kilometres, which means radio programmes can be heard up to 80 kilometres away from A.

The transmitter at B has a range of 60 kilometres.

(a) On the diagram above, show as accurately as you can the parts of the island where radio programmes can be heard.

(3)

It is planned to build a third transmitter on the island with a range of 20 kilometres.

(b) (i) Mark with an X on the diagram the best position for this transmitter.

(ii) Will this transmitter be sufficient to allow all the islanders to hear the radio programmes?

You must explain your answer.

(2)

Marks | KU | RA

9. A garden centre sells wire frames to support tall flowering plants.

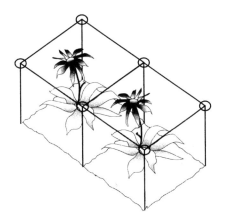

The frames consist of identical squares which are held up by metal rods through the holes at the corners.

Rows of flowers can be supported by placing squares in a straight line. Two different frames are shown in the diagram below.

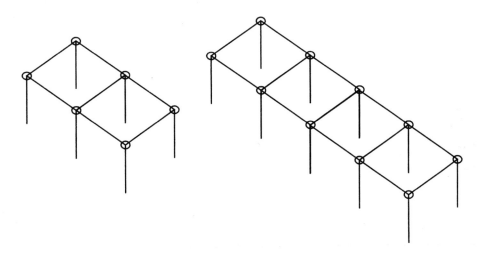

The frame with two squares needs 6 rods, one for each hole.

(*a*) Complete the table below to show the numbers of rods needed for different numbers of squares.

Number of Squares (N)	1	2	3	4	5	6
Number of Rods (R)		6				

(2)

Marks | KU | RA

(b) Write down a formula for the number of rods, R, needed for N squares.

$$R =$$

(2)

(c) Each square has a side of 30 centimetres.
How many squares and how many rods are needed to support a row of flowers 6 metres long?

(4)

10. In a school hall, the stage is lit by a spotlight fixed to a wall.
The spotlight is 4·35 metres up the wall and is set to shine on a spot on the stage 5·2 metres away from the wall, as shown in the diagram.

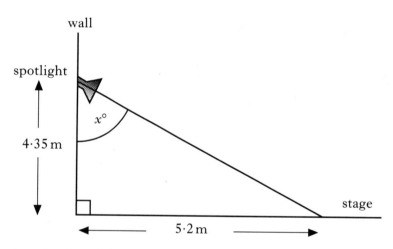

Calculate the size of the angle marked $x°$.

Do not use a scale drawing.

(4)

11. Solve the equation

$$9 + 5x = 17.$$

(2)

Marks | KU | RA

12. A wedge of cheese is in the shape of a triangular prism.
The shape and measurements of the wedge are shown in the diagram.

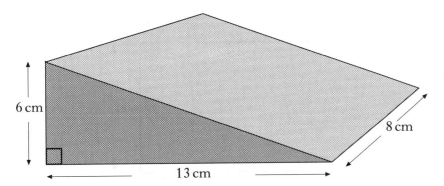

(*a*) Calculate the volume of the wedge of cheese.

(3)

(*b*) If 1 kilogram of cheese has a volume of 900 cubic centimetres, calculate the weight of the wedge of cheese in grams, giving your answer to the nearest 10 grams.

(3)

13. Factorise $15 - 10x$.

(2)

14. Brigton and Farlap are two small towns 6 kilometres apart.
A by-pass is being built to reduce the traffic passing through the two towns, as shown in the diagram.

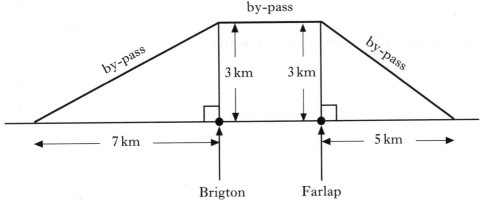

Calculate the total length of the by-pass.

(4)

Marks | KU | RA

15. A kitchen worktop is in the shape of a rectangle with a quarter-circle at one end.

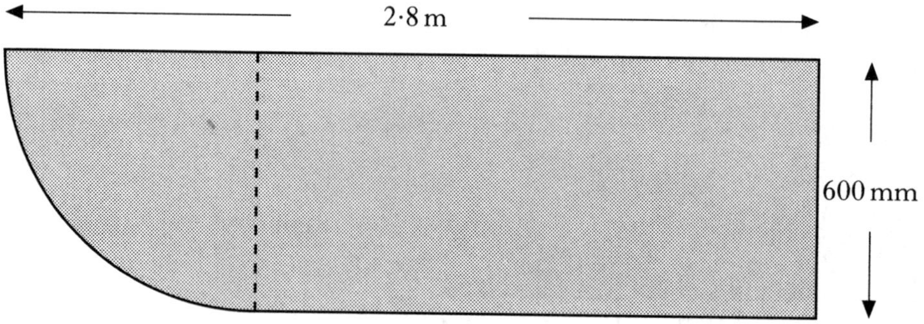

2·8 m

600 mm

The width of the worktop is 600 millimetres and the overall length is 2·8 metres, as shown in the diagram.

(*a*) What is the width of the worktop **in metres**?

(1)

(*b*) Calculate the area of the quarter-circle in square metres.

(3)

(*c*) Calculate the area of the whole worktop in square metres.

(2)

Marks | KU | RA

16.

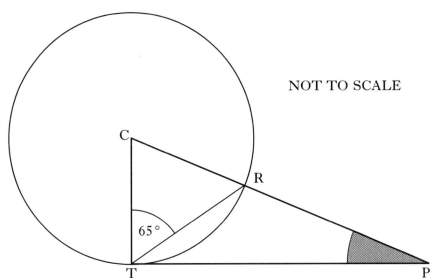

NOT TO SCALE

The diagram shows a circle with centre C.
PT is a tangent to the circle at the point T.
Angle CTR is 65°.

(*a*) Explain why angle CRT is also 65°.

(1)

(*b*) Calculate the size of the shaded angle.

(3)

17. A new cinema with 760 seats has just opened.
During the first week, the cinema was open 7 days and ran 3 showings per day.
A total of 11 530 tickets was sold.
The cinema manager has been set a target of selling at least 70% of the tickets for the first week.
Did the manager meet the target?
You must explain your answer.

[END OF QUESTION PAPER]

(4)

	Marks	KU	RA

1. Alison has invested £16 000 in a bank account which pays 6·5% interest per annum.

   She invests the money for 3 months.

   Calculate the interest she receives on her money.

   (3)

2. The average mass of a grain of pollen is $2\cdot3 \times 10^{-5}$ grams.

   Write this number out in full.

   (2)

3. The depth of a submarine was noted every three hours.

Time	noon	3 pm	6 pm	9 pm	midnight
Depth in metres	−60	−17	−28	0	−23

Complete the table below to show the change in depth of the submarine.

Time interval	Change in depth
Noon to 3 pm	up 43 metres
3 pm to 6 pm	
6 pm to 9 pm	
9 pm to midnight	

(3)

4. (*a*) On the grid below, plot the points A (−8, −3) and B (4, 6).

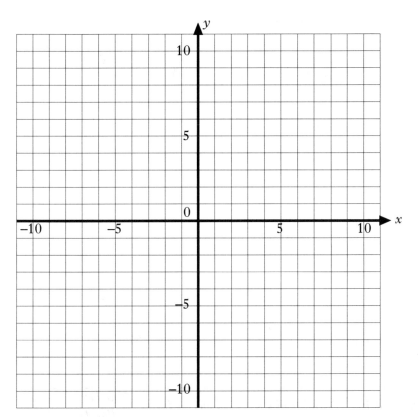

(1)

(*b*) Find the gradient of the line AB.

(2)

5. A college course is made up of 8 units of work.

Students are graded A, B, C or D on each unit.

Each grade is worth a number of points as shown in the table below.

Grade	Points
A	3
B	2
C	1
D	0

In order to pass the course, students need to

(i) complete all 8 units

and

(ii) score a total of 21 points or more.

One way is shown in the table below.

Number of As	Number of Bs	Number of Cs	Number of Ds	Number of Points
7	–	–	1	21

Fill in the rest of the table to show all the different ways of passing the course. **(4)**

Marks | KU | RA

6. Shareen works flexitime in an office. This means that she can choose her starting and finishing times each day.

One week she plans to leave work early on Friday so she works the following hours on Monday to Thursday.

Day of the Week	Start Time	Finish Time	Time Taken for Lunch
Monday	9.00 am	5.30 pm	45 minutes
Tuesday	9.00 am	5.30 pm	45 minutes
Wednesday	9.00 am	5.30 pm	45 minutes
Thursday	9.00 am	5.30 pm	45 minutes

Note: Lunchtimes are not counted as part of working hours.

On Friday she starts work at 9.00 am and does not take a lunch break.

If Shareen wants to work exactly 35 hours this week, when should she leave work on Friday?

(4)

7. The diagram below shows the shape of a traffic sign.

It consists of a rectangle and a triangle.

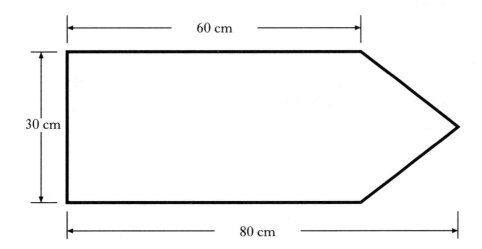

Calculate the area of the shape.

(5)

Marks | KU | RA

8. Alan and David are brothers.

Their journeys from home to school are shown on the graph below.

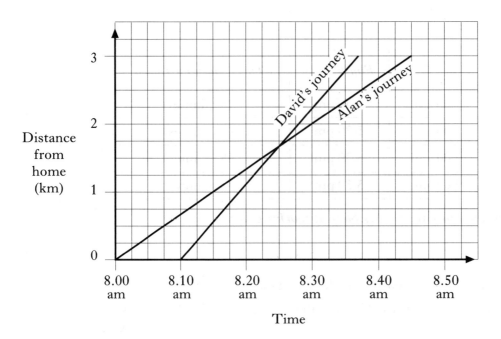

(*a*) At what time do the brothers meet on their way to school?

(1)

(*b*) How far is the school from their home?

(1)

(*c*) Calculate Alan's average speed for the journey.

Give your answer in kilometres per hour.

(4)

Marks | KU | RA

9. The sketch below shows the journey of a ship from a harbour.

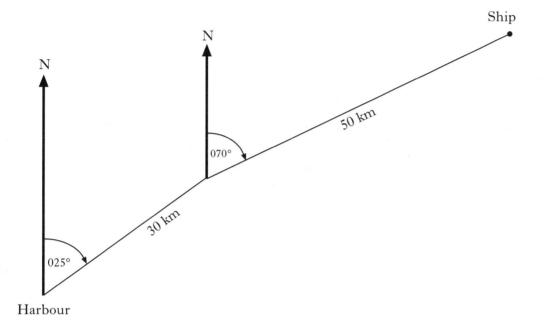

The ship leaves the harbour and sails a distance of 30 kilometres on a bearing of 025° and then sails for 50 kilometres on a bearing of 070°.

(a) Make a scale drawing of the ship's course.

Use the scale **1 cm represents 5 km**.

(3)

(b) Use your scale drawing to find the actual distance of the ship from the harbour.

(2)

10. The number squares below have **L-outlines** drawn on them.

1	2	3	4	5	6	7
8	9	10	11	12	13	14
15	16	17	18	19	20	21
22	23	24	25	26	27	28
29	30	31	32	33	34	35
36	37	38	39	40	41	42
43	44	45	46	47	48	49

The number at the top of this **L-outline** is 1.

The total of the three numbers in the **L-outline** is 18, (ie 1 + 8 + 9).

1	2	3	4	5	6	7
8	9	10	11	12	13	14
15	16	17	18	19	20	21
22	23	24	25	26	27	28
29	30	31	32	33	34	35
36	37	38	39	40	41	42
43	44	45	46	47	48	49

The number at the top of this **L-outline** is 17.

The total of the three numbers in the **L-outline** is 66.

(*a*) On the second number square, draw the **L-outline** when the number at the top is 27.

Find the total of the three numbers in this **L-outline**.

(1)

Marks | KU | RA

(b) Complete the table below.

Number at top of L-outline (N)	1	2	3	4	5	6
Total of numbers in L-outline (T)	18					

(2)

(c) Write down a formula for the total, T, of the numbers in an **L-outline** when the number at the top of the **L-outline** is N.

$$T =$$

(2)

(d) If the total in an **L-outline** is 129, find the three numbers.

(3)

11. Sunni visited France last year for seven days.

Before going on holiday she changed her £150 into French francs.

The rate of exchange was 8·5 francs to the £.

On holiday she spent 100 francs each day.

When she returned home she changed the remaining francs back into pounds.

The rate of exchange was 9·2 francs to the £.

She was charged £4 for changing the francs back into pounds.

How much did Sunni receive?

(5)

Marks KU RA

12. Crossflags golf club has a new logo.

It is formed by rotating the shape in the diagram through 90° about the point marked O.

Complete the logo.

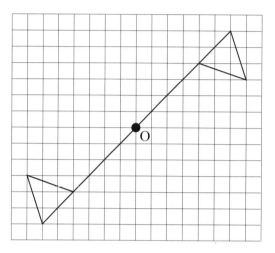

(3)

13. The diagram below shows a kite PQRS and a circle with centre Q.

PS is the tangent to the circle at P and RS is the tangent to the circle at R.

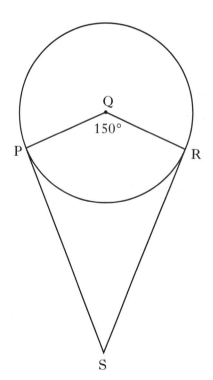

(*a*) What is the size of angle QRS?

(1)

(*b*) Calculate the size of angle PSR

(2)

Marks | KU | RA

14. A group of hillwalkers decided to climb a hill.

The graph shows their speed from the start of their climb until they reached the top of the hill.

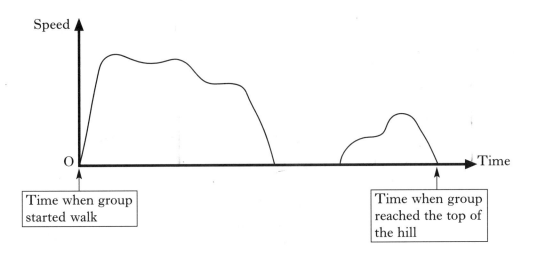

Two hours after starting the climb, the group stopped for lunch.

Use the graph to estimate how long the group stopped for lunch.

(3)

15. The percentage of softening agents in any fabric conditioner must be between 15% and 30% for it to be effective.

A 640 ml sample of Ocean, a new fabric conditioner, was found to contain 128 ml of softening agents.

Is Ocean an effective fabric conditioner?

Give a reason for your answer.

(3)

16. The sketch below shows a ramp at the back of a removal van.

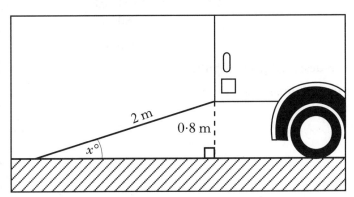

The ramp is 2 metres long and is fixed to the van 0·8 metres above the ground.

Calculate the size of the angle marked $x°$.

(4)

Marks | KU | RA

17. (*a*) Multiply out the bracket and simplify

$$5(3x + 2y) - 4x.$$

(2)

(*b*) Solve algebraically the equation

$$7x + 3 = 2x + 15.$$

(3)

18.

A dairy produces a 500 gram pack of butter in the shape of a cylinder.

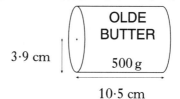

3·9 cm

10·5 cm

The radius of the circular end of the pack is 3·9 centimetres and the length of the pack is 10·5 centimetres.

(*a*) Calculate the volume of the pack of butter.

Give your answer to the nearest whole number.

(3)

The 500 gram pack is redesigned. It is now produced in the shape of a cuboid with a square end of side 6·5 centimetres.

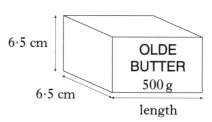

6·5 cm

6·5 cm

length

(*b*) Calculate the length of the redesigned pack of butter.

Give your answer correct to 1 decimal place.

(3)

19. (*a*) A rectangular picture measuring 610 millimetres by 180 millimetres is placed diagonally in a cuboid shaped box as shown in Diagram 1.

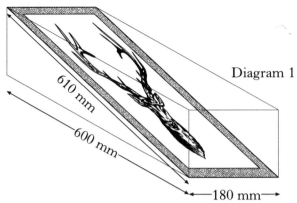

Diagram 1

The box has length 600 millimetres and breadth 180 millimetres.

Calculate the height of the box.

(3)

(*b*) An international parcel delivery service accepts cuboid shaped parcels as shown in Diagram 2 provided L + B + H does not exceed 900 millimetres.

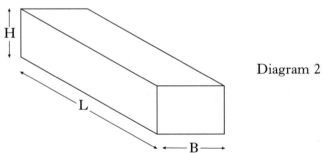

Diagram 2

Will the box in part (*a*) be accepted by the parcel delivery service?

You must explain your answer.

(2)

[END OF QUESTION PAPER]

SCOTTISH
CERTIFICATE OF
EDUCATION
1997

FRIDAY, 9 MAY
10.50 AM – 12.20 PM

MATHEMATICS
STANDARD GRADE
General Level

Marks | KU | RA

1. The brightest star in the sky has a diameter of 2·33 million kilometres.

    (a) Write 2·33 million in figures.

    (1)

    (b) Write 2·33 million in scientific notation.

    (1)

2. During one week in winter, the midday temperatures in Oban were as shown.

Sunday	−1 °C
Monday	−2 °C
Tuesday	−3 °C
Wednesday	4 °C
Thursday	3 °C
Friday	0 °C
Saturday	6 °C

    Calculate the average of these temperatures.

    (3)

Marks KU RA

3. Adam works in a factory.

He works a basic week of 39 hours.

He is paid £4·80 per hour.

All overtime is paid at time and a half.

(*a*) One week Adam works 46 hours.

Calculate his gross pay.

(4)

(*b*) Adam should start work at 8 am.

Part of Adam's time card for one week is shown.

ADAM ROSS	START
MONDAY	0810
TUESDAY	0755
WEDNESDAY	0807
THURSDAY	0746
FRIDAY	0805

Each day his time card is checked. He loses a quarter of an hour's basic pay for **every 15 minutes, or part of 15 minutes,** that he arrives late.

How much money does Adam lose for being late this week?

(3)

4. Heather has a security lock for her mountain bicycle. The lock has a 3-digit code.

Each digit can be 1, 2, 3, 4 or 5.

For example, the code on this lock is 212.

On Heather's lock,

• the first digit is a prime number greater than 3

• the sum of the three digits is greater than 12.

Write down all the possible codes for Heather's lock.

(3)

Marks | KU | RA

5. A mobile phone company lists its charges as follows.

Phone Rental	£12·75 per month
Peak rate calls	42p per minute
Off-peak calls	18p per minute
+ VAT at 17·5%	

Complete this phone bill.

Rental for 1 month   £12·75

296 minutes at peak rate   £

183 minutes at off-peak rate   £

VAT at 17·5 %   £

TOTAL

(5)

6. Anwar is making a bookcase.

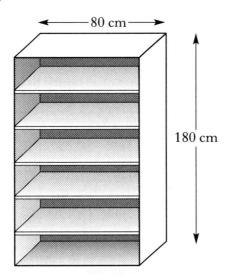

The back of the bookcase is rectangular in shape and measures 180 centimetres by 80 centimetres.

To make the bookcase stronger, Anwar is going to attach a metal strip along one of the diagonals at the back.

He has a metal strip that is 2 metres long.

Is the strip long enough to fit along the diagonal?

Give a reason for your answer

(4)

Marks | KU | RA

7. (*a*) On the grid below, plot the points

$$A(1, 6), \quad B(4, -2) \quad \text{and} \quad C(1, -4).$$

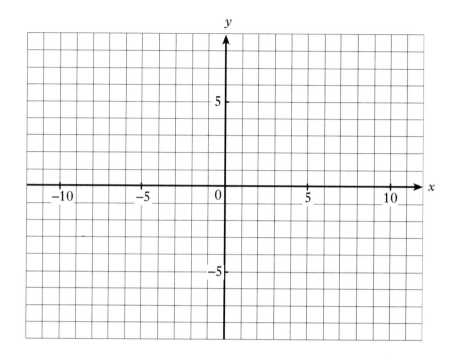

(1)

(*b*) Plot the point D so that ABCD forms a kite.

(1)

(*c*) Find the gradient of the line AB.

(2)

8. A bathroom mat is shown below.

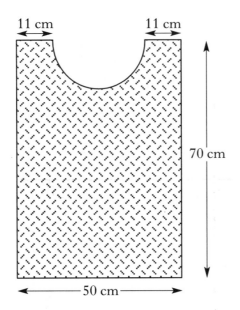

11 cm   11 cm

70 cm

50 cm

The shape is a rectangle with a semi-circle cut out.

Calculate the area of the mat.

(4)

Marks | KU | RA

9. An ornamental garden fence is made by joining posts with two chains as shown below.

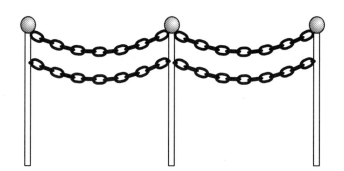

This fence
has 3 posts
and 4 chains.

(a) Complete the following table.

Number of posts (P)	1	2	3	4		20
Number of chains (C)	0		4			

(2)

(b) Write down a formula for the number of chains, C, when you know the number of posts, P.

$$C =$$

(2)

(c) Sally has 18 posts and 31 chains.

What is the largest number of posts and the largest number of chains that she can use to make the same type of fence?

(3)

Marks | KU | RA

10. Tom and Anna set off from their campsite and walk for 8 km on a bearing of 035°.

They stop for a break.

They then walk for 6 km in a south-easterly direction.

(*a*) Using a scale of **1 cm to 1 km**, make a scale drawing of their journey.

Campsite

(3)

(*b*) **Use your scale drawing** to find the bearing they should take to return to the campsite.

(2)

11. Last year a record company advertised in magazines, on radio and on television.

The total spent on advertising was £34 000 000.

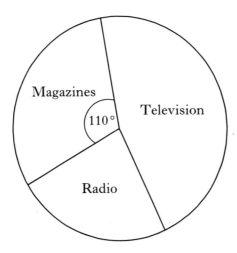

Use the pie chart to calculate the amount of money spent on advertising in magazines.

Round your answer to the nearest million pounds.

(3)

Marks | KU | RA

12. The diagram below shows a yacht with a mast of height **X** metres.

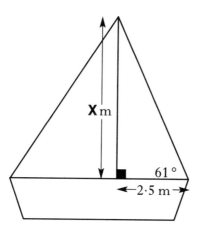

Calculate the height of the yacht's mast.
Do not use a scale drawing.

(4)

13. Sophia owns a paint shop.

She displays tins of paint as shown below.

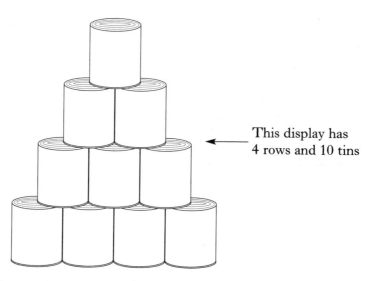

This display has
4 rows and 10 tins

Each tin is 15 centimetres high.

Sophia wants the display to be 1·05 metres high.

How many tins of paint will she need?

(5)

Marks | KU | RA

14. (*a*) Solve algebraically

$$6x - 2 \geq 17.$$

(2)

(*b*) Factorise fully

$$12ab - 8c.$$

(2)

15. The shape below is rotated through $180°$ about **X**.

Draw the shape in its new position.

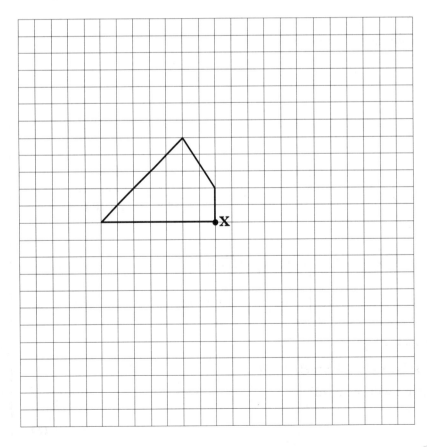

(3)

16.

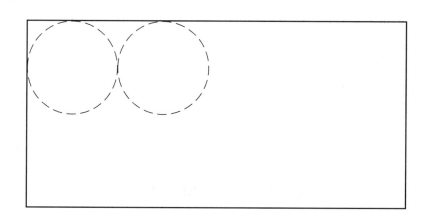

Circular plates are cut from a rectangular sheet of metal.

The area, *A*, of each plate is 340 cm².

(*a*) Use the formula $r = \sqrt{\dfrac{A}{\pi}}$ to calculate the radius, *r*, of the plate.

(3)

(*b*) Can 3 of these plates be cut from a sheet of metal measuring 60 centimetres by 21 centimetres?

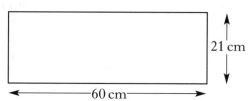

21 cm

60 cm

Give a reason for your answer.

(4)

Marks | KU | RA

17. The cost, £C, of a taxi journey varies directly as the distance, D miles, travelled.

A 12 mile journey costs £10·20.

Find the cost of a 17 mile journey.

(4)

18.

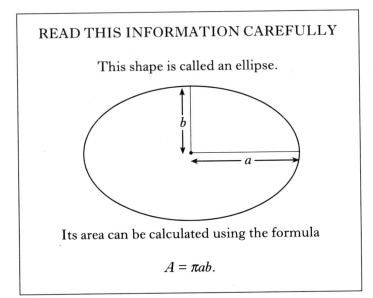

READ THIS INFORMATION CAREFULLY

This shape is called an ellipse.

Its area can be calculated using the formula

$A = \pi ab.$

The figure opposite shows a breakfast cereal container.

The height of the container is 30 centimetres.

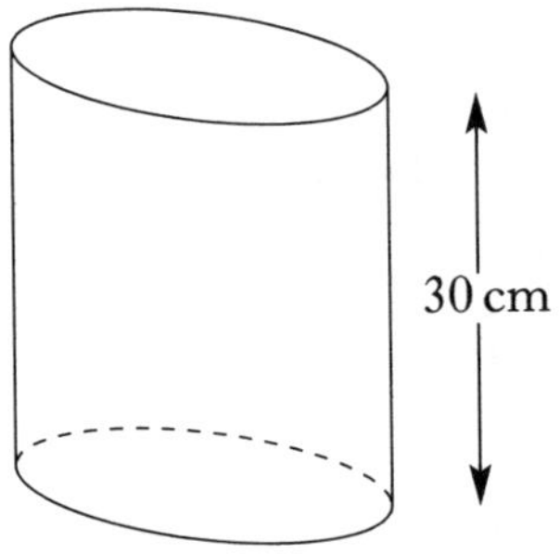

30 cm

The base of the container is an ellipse 16 centimetres long and 8 centimetres wide.

Calculate the volume of the container.

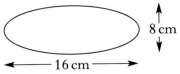

8 cm

16 cm

[END OF QUESTION PAPER]

(4)

SCOTTISH
CERTIFICATE OF
EDUCATION
1998

FRIDAY, 8 MAY
10.50 AM – 12.20 PM

MATHEMATICS
STANDARD GRADE
General Level

Marks | KU | RA

1. The temperature recorded at 6 am in Aviemore is shown on the diagram below.

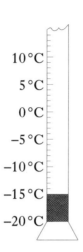

(*a*) By 9 am, the temperature had risen to −7 °C.

By how many degrees had the temperature risen?

(1)

(*b*) By 2 pm, the temperature had risen by a further 9 degrees.

What was the temperature at 2 pm?

(1)

Marks | KU | RA

2. One video costs £13·50.

On Special Offer is a set of 8 videos costing £104.

1 VIDEO — £13·50

SPECIAL OFFER

8-VIDEO SET—£104

(a) How much is saved by buying the set?

(2)

(b) Express the saving as a percentage of the cost of 8 single videos.

(2)

3. To raise money for its funds, a school organises a competition.

In this competition, each person selects **10** football teams.

Points are awarded as follows.

Points

	Points
Win	3
Score Draw	2
No-Score Draw	1
Loss	0

PRIZES ARE AWARDED
FOR **27 POINTS OR MORE**

One way of winning a prize is shown in the table below.

Number of teams getting 3 points	Number of teams getting 2 points	Number of teams getting 1 point	Number of teams getting 0 points	Total number of points
9	0	1	0	28
8	1	1	0	27
7	3	0	0	27
10	0	0	0	30
9	1	0	0	29
8	2	0	0	28
9	0	0	1	27

Complete the table to show all the different ways of winning a prize.

(4)

Marks | KU | RA

4. Michael's monthly salary is £720.

He spends $\frac{1}{5}$ of this on his mortgage, $\frac{3}{20}$ on his car and $\frac{1}{10}$ on insurance.

He uses the remainder for his household expenses.

(a) How much money does he spend on his car each month?

(1)

(b) What fraction of his monthly salary does he use for household expenses?

(2)

5.

EXCHANGE RATES for £1 Sterling

FRANCE	8·92	francs
GERMANY	2·65	marks
GREECE	426	drachmas
ITALY	2650	lire
SPAIN	220	pesetas

(a) Scott goes on holiday to Spain.

He buys a camera costing 9900 pesetas.

How much is this in pounds sterling?

(2)

(b) The same camera costs 121·9 marks in Germany and 18531 drachmas in Greece.

In which of the three countries is the camera cheapest?

(3)

Marks | KU | RA

6. Solve **algebraically** the inequality

$$7y + 3 < 24.$$

(2)

7. New York time is 5 hours behind British time.

When it is 7 pm in Britain, it is 2 pm in New York.

(a) At 10 am Gordon, who is in New York, phones home to Britain. What time is it in Britain?

(1)

(b) Los Angeles time is 3 hours behind New York time.

From Los Angeles, Fiona needs to phone a colleague in Aberdeen before 6 pm, British time.

She makes the phone call at 9.30 am, Los Angeles time.

Does she meet the 6 pm deadline?

Give a reason for your answer.

(4)

8.

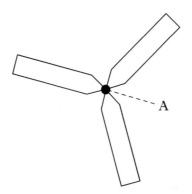

The logo above has rotational symmetry of **order 3** about point A.

Part of a company logo is shown below.

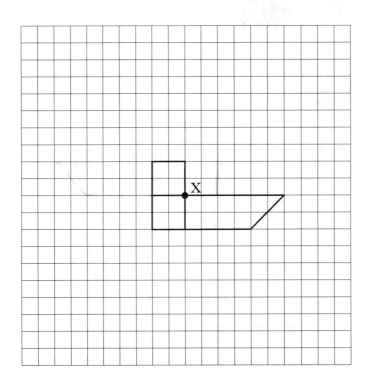

Complete the logo so that it has rotational symmetry of order 4 about point X.   **(3)**

Marks | KU | RA

9. The table below shows the distance in miles between different places in Scotland.

EDINBURGH
48	GLASGOW			
158	165	INVERNESS		
45	62	113	PERTH	
56	8	173	70	PAISLEY
124	85	250	145	75	STRANRAER

(*a*) Use the table above to find the distance from Edinburgh to Paisley.

(1)

(*b*) Allan is a salesman whose office is in Edinburgh.

He gets travelling expenses at the rate of 27·5 pence per mile.

On Monday he travels from Edinburgh to Paisley and back.

How much does he get in travelling expenses?

(2)

(*c*) Each year, **after** he has travelled 8000 miles, Allan's expenses are reduced to 16·2 pence per mile.

In 1997, Allan travelled 9200 miles altogether.

What were his **total** travelling expenses for 1997?

(3)

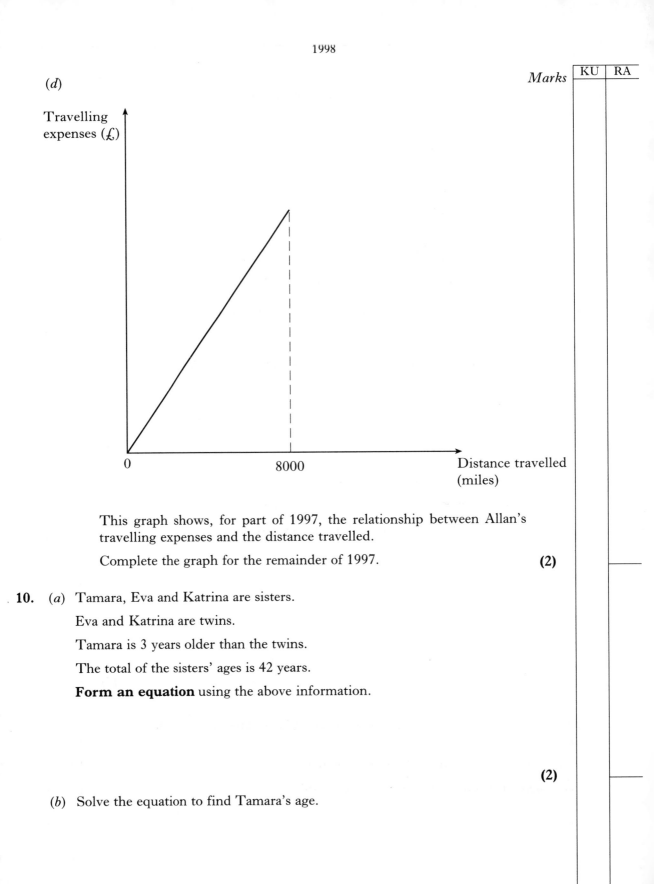

(d)

Travelling expenses (£)

0   8000   Distance travelled (miles)

This graph shows, for part of 1997, the relationship between Allan's travelling expenses and the distance travelled.

Complete the graph for the remainder of 1997.

(2)

10. (a) Tamara, Eva and Katrina are sisters.

Eva and Katrina are twins.

Tamara is 3 years older than the twins.

The total of the sisters' ages is 42 years.

Form an equation using the above information.

(2)

(b) Solve the equation to find Tamara's age.

(2)

Marks | KU | RA

11. A wall display cabinet is made in the shape of an equilateral triangle with length of side 40 centimetres.

One half of the cabinet has shelves; the other half has a glass door.

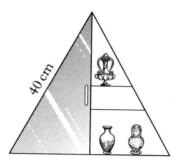

(*a*) Calculate the height of the cabinet.

(4)

(*b*) Find the area of the glass door.

(2)

Marks | KU | RA

12.

A milk carton is in the shape of a cuboid with a square base.

The sides of the base are 8 centimetres long.

(*a*) The volume of the carton is 1280 cubic centimetres.

What is the height of the carton?

(2)

(*b*) A second cuboid carton, which also has a square base, holds 1·75 litres of milk.

The height of this carton is 25 cm.

Find the length of the base.

(3)

Marks | KU | RA

13. Factorise $15w + 6st$.

(2)

14. Superbuy Stores have a Friendly card which allows a shopper to collect points for money spent.

One point is given for each whole £1 spent.

(a) Anjum spends £27·26 in a Superbuy Store.

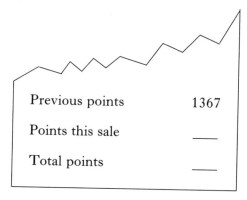

Previous points   1367

Points this sale   ____

Total points   ____

Complete his till receipt.

(2)

(b) When you buy petrol from Superbuy, you get 3 points for every £5 spent.

Points may be exchanged for goods.

How much must be spent on petrol to obtain a personal stereo worth 380 points?

(3)

Marks | KU | RA

15. The line AB is drawn on the coordinate diagram below.

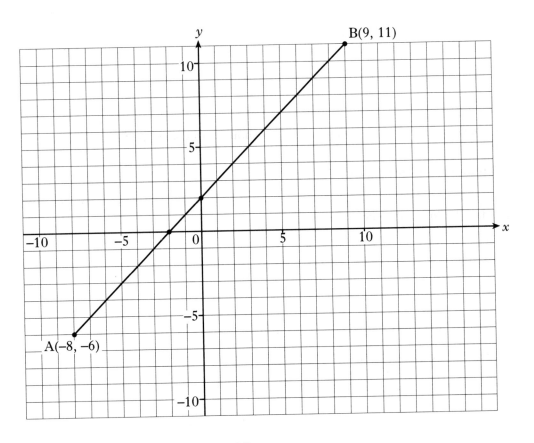

(*a*) Find the gradient of the line AB.

(2)

(*b*) On the same coordinate diagram, draw the line with equation $y = 2x - 4$.

(2)

16. In the park, two new flower beds are being planted with roses.

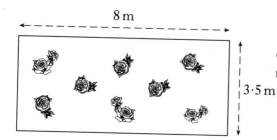

8 m

3·5 m

One flower bed is rectangular and measures 8 metres by 3·5 metres.

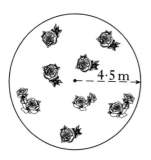

4·5 m

The other is circular with a radius of 4·5 metres.

(a) A fence is to be put around **each** flower bed.

Find the **total** length of fencing required.

(3)

(b) Fencing is sold by the metre.

What is the minimum length of fencing which must be bought?

(1)

Marks KU RA

Marks | KU | RA

17. The sides of a bridge are constructed by joining sections.

The sections are made of steel girders.

1 section
3 girders

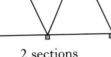
2 sections
7 girders

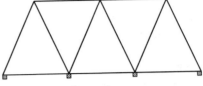
3 sections

(a) Complete the table below.

Number of sections (s)	1	2	3	4		10
Number of girders (g)	3	7				

(2)

(b) Write down a formula for the number of girders, *g*, when you know the number of sections, *s*.

(2)

(c) Each section is an isosceles triangle.

The base is 11·25 metres long. The other girders are 15·65 metres long.

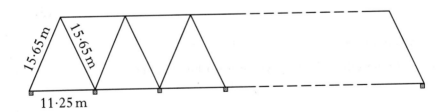
15·65 m
15·65 m
11·25 m

What is the total length of girders required for **one** side of a bridge 90 metres long?

(4)

18.

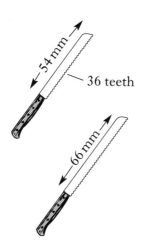

54 mm

36 teeth

66 mm

The blade of a knife is 54 millimetres long.

The blade has 36 teeth.

The blade of a larger knife is 66 millimetres long.

The ratio $\dfrac{\text{number of teeth}}{\text{length of blade}}$ is the same for both knives.

How many teeth does the larger knife have?

(2)

19. The design of a trolley wheel is shown.

The manufacturer requires that **angle x must be more than 32°**.

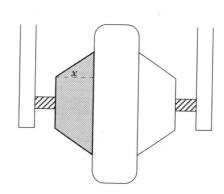

x

Part of this design has measurements as shown.

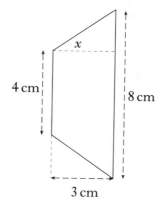

x

4 cm

8 cm

3 cm

Do these measurements satisfy the manufacturer's requirements?

Give a reason for your answer.

Do not use a scale drawing.

(4)

Marks | KU | RA

Marks | KU | RA

20.

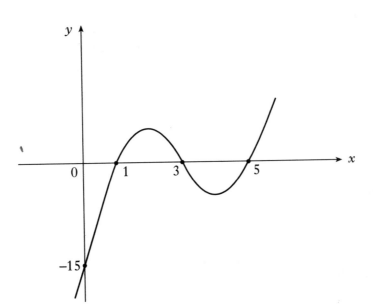

The diagram above shows the graph whose equation is $y = (x-1)(x-3)(x-5)$.

Write down an equation for each of the graphs below.

(*a*)

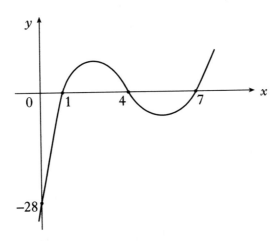

(1)

(b)

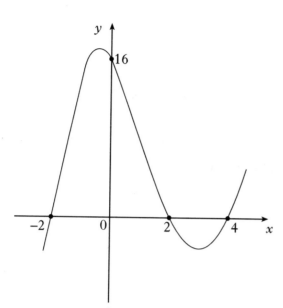

(2)

[*END OF QUESTION PAPER*]

SCOTTISH
CERTIFICATE OF
EDUCATION
1999

WEDNESDAY, 5 MAY
10.50 AM – 12.20 PM

6.25
7.25

MATHEMATICS
STANDARD GRADE
General Level

Marks | KU | RA
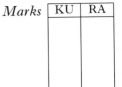

1. The cost of hiring a Yellow Taxi consists of a basic charge plus a charge per kilometre.

The cost of journeys up to 10 kilometres is shown in the graph below.

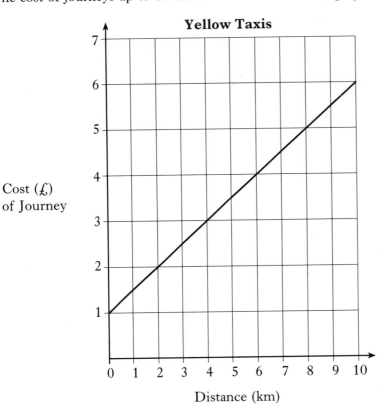

(*a*) How much is the basic charge?

£1

(1)

(*b*) How much do Yellow Taxis charge per kilometre?

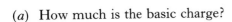
50p per kilometre.

(2)

(*c*) Find the cost of a 12 kilometre taxi journey.

11 – £6.50
12 – £7.

(2)

| | Marks | KU | RA |

2. Mr and Mrs Donaldson are having a party to celebrate their 25th Wedding Anniversary.

They want to buy Champagne.

They see this sign in a shop window.

CHAMPAGNE

£24·99 per bottle

15% Discount when you buy 6 bottles

Calculate the cost of 6 bottles.

£24.99 × 6 = £149.99 × 15% = £22.49

£149.99 - £22.49 = £127.45

(3)

3. (a) Draw the next T-shape in this sequence.

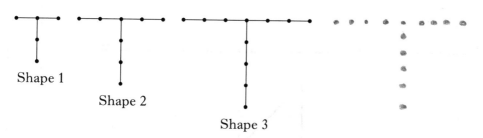

Shape 1

Shape 2

Shape 3

Shape 4

(1)

(b) Complete the following table.

Shape Number (s)	1	2	3	4	5		16
Number of dots (d)	5	8	11	14	17		50

3   3   3   3

(2)

(c) Write down a formula for the number of dots (d) when you know the shape number (s).

$d = 3 \; s + 2$

(2)

(d) 101 dots are used in drawing a T-shape.

What is its shape number?

$101 = 3s + 2$

z 101 ÷ 3 = 33

(2)

Marks | KU | RA

4. Ticketmasters Call Centre can handle 240 calls for concert tickets every 2 hours.

How many calls can they handle in 45 minutes?

$240 \div 2 = 120$ calls

$120 \div 4 = 30$ calls $\times 3 = 90$ calls in 45 mins.

(2)

5. The two shapes below are reflected in the line AB.

Draw the new positions of the two shapes.

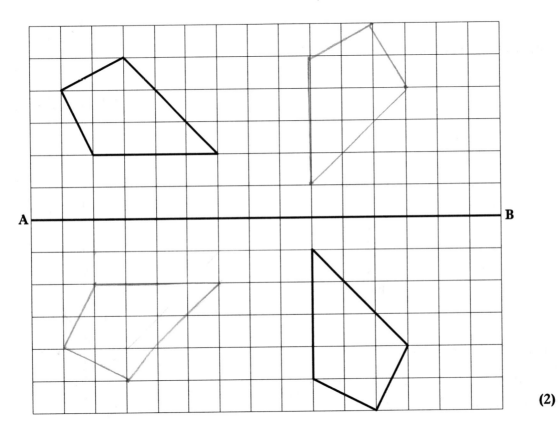

(2)

6.

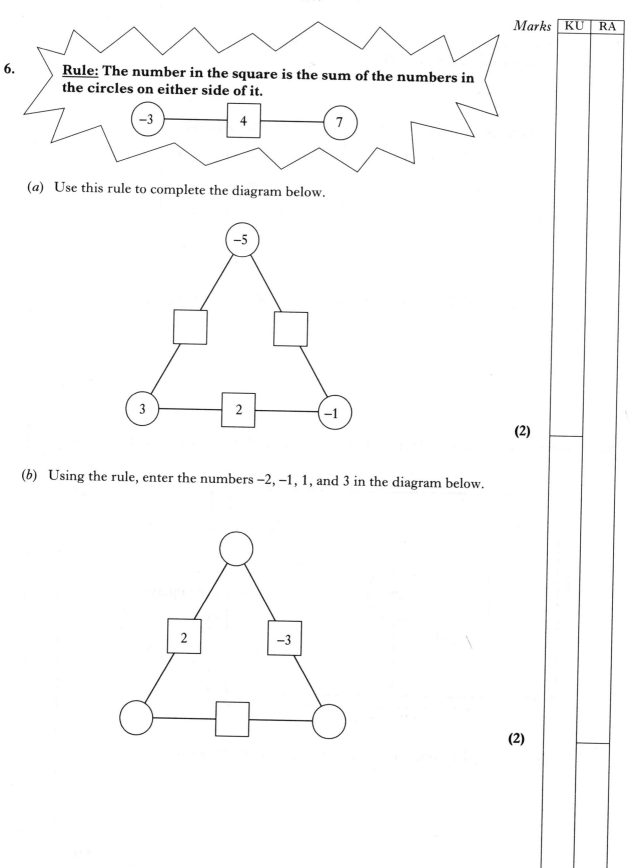

Rule: The number in the square is the sum of the numbers in the circles on either side of it.

(−3) — [4] — (7)

(a) Use this rule to complete the diagram below.

(−5) at top
[ ] [ ]
(3) — [2] — (−1)

(2)

(b) Using the rule, enter the numbers −2, −1, 1, and 3 in the diagram below.

( ) at top
[2] [−3]
( ) — [ ] — ( )

(2)

Marks KU RA

7. Two lenders, Mortgages Direct and Leading Mortgage, offer mortgages at different rates on a loan of £45 000.

Mortgages Direct

Monthly payment £330·50

Plus

One-off set-up fee £500

Leading Mortgage

Monthly payment £349·90

And

No other fees to pay

Which mortgage would be better value over a period of 3 years and by how much?

(5)

8. A football pitch used in the Premier League measures 105 metres by 68 metres.

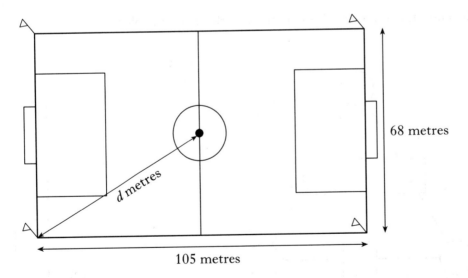

68 metres

d metres

105 metres

Find the distance, *d* metres, from the corner flag to the centre spot.

(4)

Marks | KU | RA

9. (*a*) Complete the table below for $y = 3x + 1$.

x	-3	0	3
y			

(2)

(*b*) Using the table in part (*a*), draw the graph of the line $y = 3x + 1$ on the grid below.

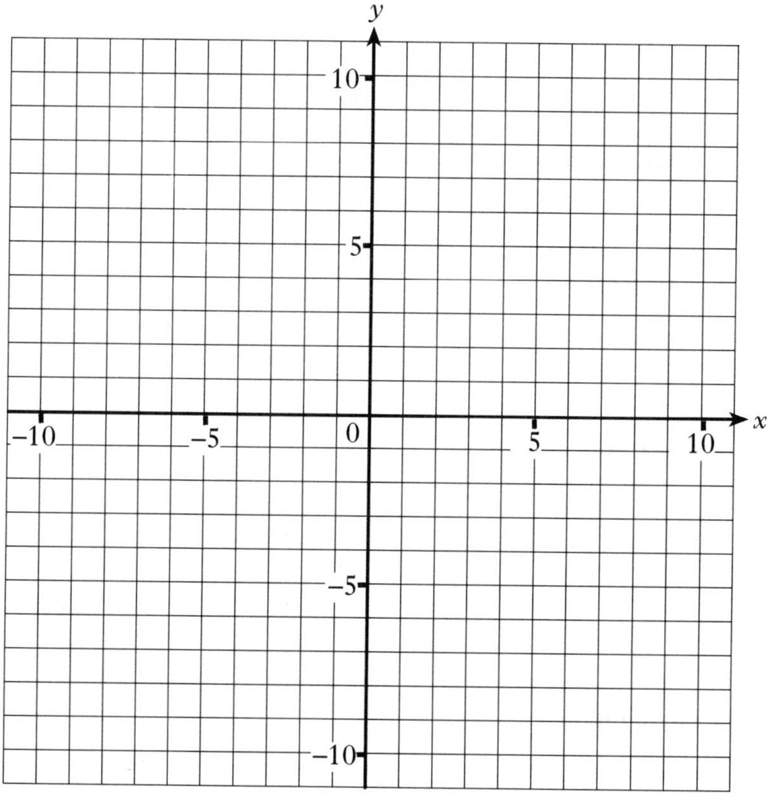

(2)

10.

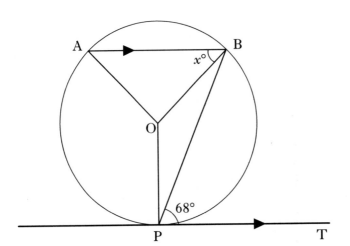

PT is a tangent to the circle, centre O.

PT is parallel to AB.

Angle BPT = 68°.

(*a*) What is the size of the angle BPO?

(1)

(*b*) Calculate the size of the angle marked $x°$.

(3)

Marks | KU | RA

1. A battery operated toy train travels on a circular track.

The radius of the circle is 40 centimetres.

It takes one minute for the train to travel 8 times round the track.

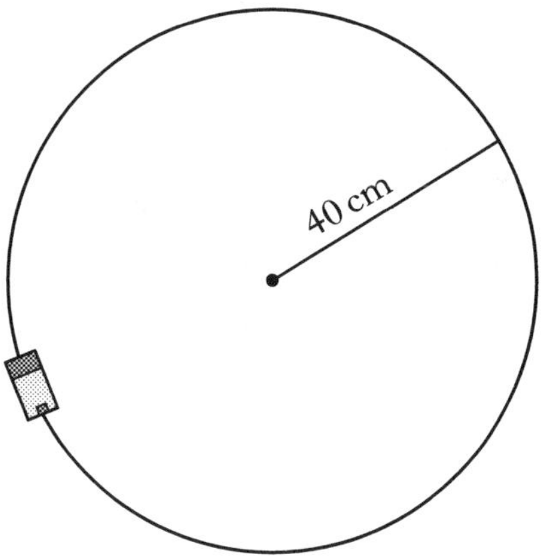

40 cm

(a) How far does the train travel in one minute?

Give your answer to the nearest 10 centimetres.

(4)

(b) Find the speed of the train in centimetres per second.

(2)

2. The angle of elevation from the ground to the top of a block of flats is 48°.

The angle is measured at a point 75 metres from the flats as shown in the diagram below.

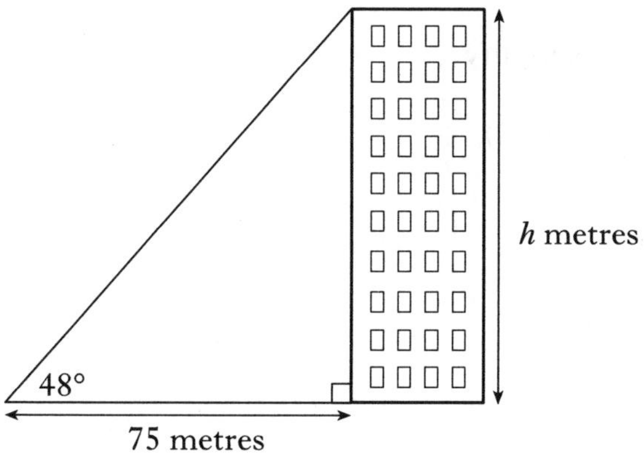

h metres

48°

75 metres

Calculate the height, h metres, of the block of flats, correct to 1 decimal place.

(4)

Marks | KU | RA

13. Amy needs to replace fencing in her garden.

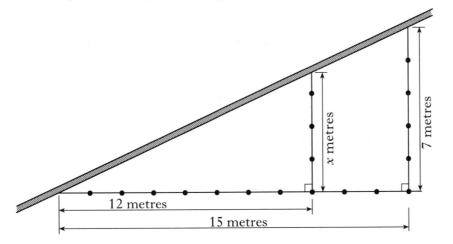

She has taken the measurements shown above, but has forgotten to measure the part of the fence marked x metres.

The garden centre has only 28 metres of fencing in stock.

Is this enough to completely replace the existing fencing?

(4)

14. (*a*) Multiply out the brackets and simplify

$$2a + 3(4a - 5).$$

(2)

(*b*) Solve **algebraically** the equation

$$4x - 3 = x + 5.$$

(3)

Marks | KU | RA

15.

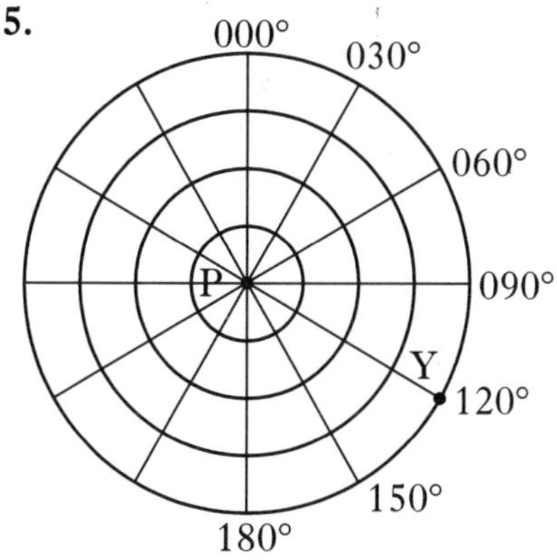

000° 030°

060°

090°

Y
120°

150°

180°

The diagram shows a Coastguard's radar screen.

The circles on the screen have radii of 10 km, 20 km, 30 km, and 40 km.

On the radar screen, port P is at the centre.

The yacht Y is also shown on the radar screen.

(a) Plot the position of yacht Y on the map.

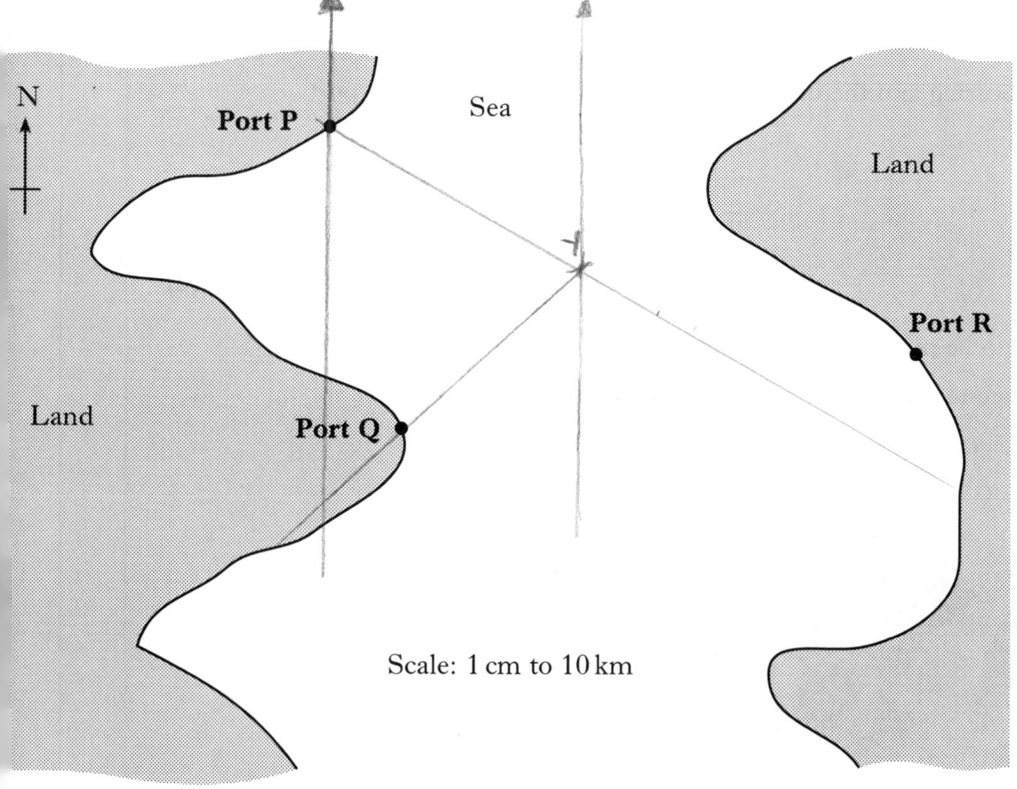

N

Port P

Sea

Land

Port R

Land

Port Q

Scale: 1 cm to 10 km

(2)

Marks KU RA

(b) The Coastguard receives a warning of bad weather and advises the yacht to sail to the nearest port.

To which port should the yacht sail?

Give a reason for your answer.

(2)

(c) Find the bearing and the distance from the yacht to the nearest port.

(2)

16. A sculpture is to be made by stacking three blocks of stone.

Each block of stone is a cube of side $(1{\cdot}2 \pm 0{\cdot}05)$ metres.

What is the maximum height of the sculpture?

(2)

Marks | KU | RA

17. A pattern of circular discs of **diameter 6 centimetres** is to be cut from a square sheet of plastic.

The diagram below shows part of this sheet.

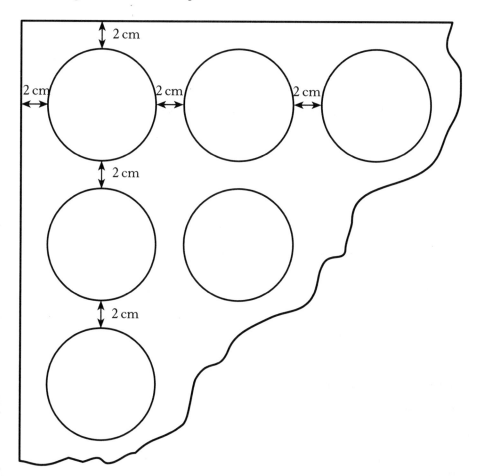

(a) How many circular discs could be cut from a square sheet of plastic of side 50 centimetres?

(3)

(b) Find the area of plastic remaining after the discs have been cut from the square sheet.

(4)

Marks | KU | RA

18. The distance to the horizon, d kilometres, varies as the square root of the height, h metres, above sea level.

The distance to the horizon is 14·4 kilometres at a height of 16 metres above sea level.

Calculate the distance to the horizon at a height of 25 metres above sea level.

(4)

19.

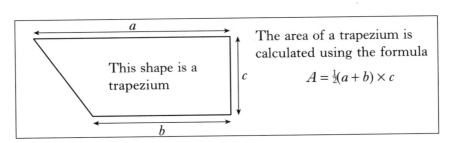

The area of a trapezium is calculated using the formula

$$A = \tfrac{1}{2}(a + b) \times c$$

This shape is a trapezium

The diagram below shows part of a rainwater gutter.

The ends of the gutter are identical.

Each end is in the shape of a trapezium.

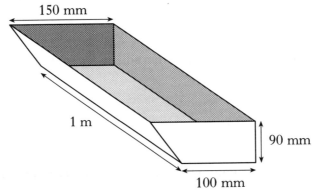

Calculate the **volume** of this part of the gutter.

(4)

[END OF QUESTION PAPER]

1. £350

2. 243

3. *(a)* 3   *(b)*

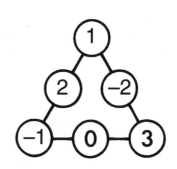

4. *(a)* 1:1000 000 (1 cm : 10 km)
(b)   *(c)* 27 km

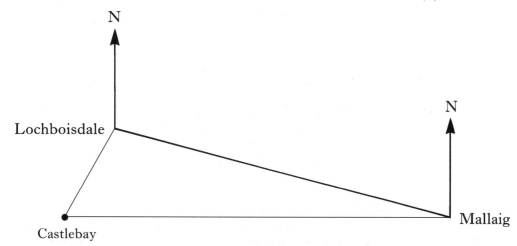

5. No; {£83 125 < £84 000}

6. *(a)* 66°   *(b)* Angle between tangent and radius   *(c)* 114°

7. *(a)* Attendances are increasing
(b) Attendances **rose** then **fell**
(c) Approx. 38 000

8. Yes; {71° < A < 76°}

9. *(a)*

Number of miles	0	250	500	750	1000	1250	1500
"FREEDOM": cost in £	205	205	205	205	205	205	205
"ROVER": cost in £	145	160	175	190	205	220	235

(b) (i) & (ii)

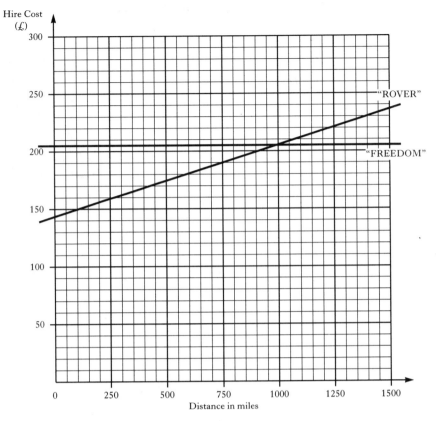

(c) Freedom scheme would be better. (It is £24 cheaper.)

10. *(a)* (i) $2x$ (ii) $x - 12$ *(b)* $2x + x - 12 + x = 80$; $x = 23$ **11.** *(a)* 64   *(b)* 320 cm

12. *(a)*

x	−4	0	4
y	−7	1	9

(b)

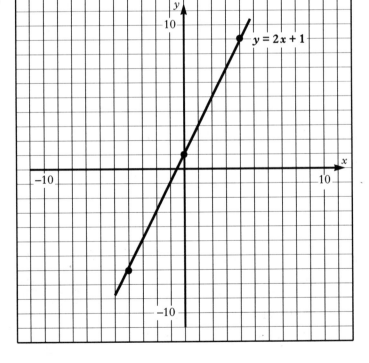

(c) gradient = 2

13. When data is plotted on a graph it forms a straight line through the origin.

14. *(a)* $r = 9300$ km   *(b)* $S = 23\,400$ km/h

15. 212 cm   **16.** 87%   **17.** *(a)* 36·7 litres   *(b)* 8 supports

1. £21.46

2. *(a)* HEIGHT

    (b) Darren is taller than Alexander

    (c) See diagram

(c) • Claire

    • Darren

      • Alexander

AGE

3. Area = 644 cm^2

4. *(a)*

Number of Pack A	Number of Pack B	Number of Pack C
	1	2
		3
	2	1
1		2
	3	
1	1	1

    (b) 1 pack of A and 2 packs of C a total of 15 photographs

5. *(a)* Angle = 100°   *(b)* Amount ≐ £24 million

6. They should use Wilson and Lyle as they are £50 cheaper

7. Distance ≐ 10·3 km   **8.** R = 1·83

9. *(a)*   *(b)* See diagram, point (1, 5)

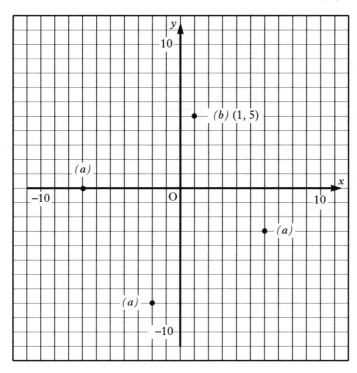

10. *(a)* At £1.623 Coverite is the least cost per litre   *(b)* Tuffcote
11. H = 4·90 m
12. 10 hours 15 minutes
13. *(a)* 3 times   *(b)* depth = 90 cm   *(c)* volume = 1620 litres
14. $x < 6$
15. *(a)* map distance = 5·6 cm   *(b)* actual distance = 2·8 km
16. *(a)* perimeter = 388·4 m   *(b)* L = 168 m
17. YES; since the slope {0·05} is less than 0·07
18. 99 tonnes needed
19. *(a)* R4 is 4 cm × 5 cm
    (b) Four R4 pieces can be cut from an R10 piece {R10 is 10 cm × 11 cm}

1995 — GENERAL LEVEL ANSWERS

1. 382 400 Lire   2. *(a)* 11 °C   *(b)* −9 °C   3. 230
4. *(a)* 2229   *(b)* 4443
        3336
        4443
        5550
5. *(a)* 15 hours 36 minutes   *(b)* Winter. In winter, darkness falls in the afternoon.
6. *(a)* 50 packets   *(b)* 66 cm   *(c)* 7 boxes   7. *(a)* £56   *(b)* £2.50
8. *(a)* On diagram {Scale drawing}
   (b) (i) On diagram
        (ii) Yes; since the whole island covered

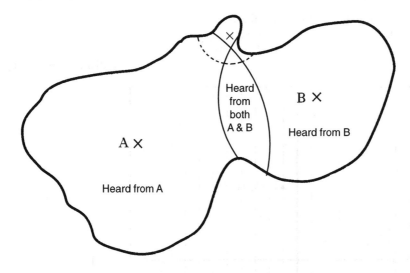

9. *(a)*

Number of Squares (N)	1	2	3	4	5	6
Number of Rods (R)	4	6	8	10	12	14

    (b) $R = 2N + 2$ *(c)* 20 squares and 42 rods

10. 50·1°

11. $\frac{8}{5}$ or 1·6

12. *(a)* 312 cm^3 *(b)* 350 g

13. $5(3 - 2x)$

14. 19·45 km

15. *(a)* 0·6 m *(b)* 0·3 m^2 *(c)* 1·6 m^2

16. *(a)* Isosceles triangle *(b)* 40°

17. YES; since 11 530 > 11 172 (70% of 15 960)

1996 — GENERAL LEVEL ANSWERS

1. £260

2. 0·000023

3.

Time interval	Change in depth
Noon to 3 pm	up 43 metres
3 pm to 6 pm	Down 11 metres
6 pm to 9 pm	Up 28 metres
9 pm to midnight	Down 23 metres

4. *(a)*

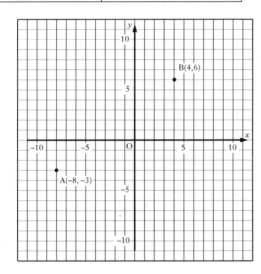

    (b) $\frac{3}{4}$

5.

Number of As	Number of Bs	Number of Cs	Number of Ds	Number of Points
7	–	–	1	21
5	3	–	–	21
6	1	1	–	21
6	2	–	–	22
7	–	1	–	22
7	1	–	–	23
8	–	–	–	24

6. 1 pm   **7.** 2100 cm^2

8. *(a)* 8.25 am   *(b)* 3 km   *(c)* 4 k.p.h.

9. *(a)* Scale Drawing   *(b)* 15 cm : 75 km
        1 cm : 5 km

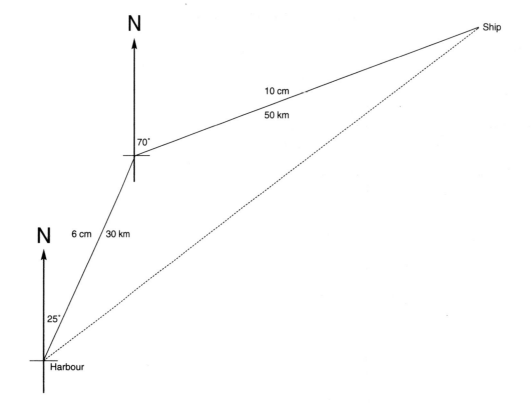

10. *(a)*

27	
34	**35**

Total = 96

(b) *Total of numbers in L -outline (T)*   18   **21**   **24**   **27**   **30**   **33**

(c) T = 3N + 15   *(d)*

38	
45	**46**

96

11. £58.50

12.

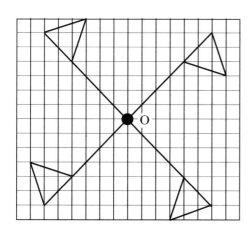

13. *(a)* 90°   *(b)* 30°

14. 40 minutes

15. Yes; since {15% < 20% < 30%}

16. 23·6°

17. *(a)* $11x + 10y$
   (b) $x = \dfrac{12}{5}$ or 2·4

18. *(a)* $V \doteqdot 501$ cm³
   (b) $l \doteqdot 11\cdot9$ cm

19. *(a)* height = 110 mm   *(b)* Yes; {Since 890 mm < 900 mm}

1. *(a)* 2 330 000   *(b)* $2 \cdot 33 \times 10^6$

2. 1 °C

3. *(a)* £237.60   *(b)* £3.60

4. 555; 554; 553; 545; 535; 544

5. £124.32; £32.94; {£170.01}; vat £29.75; total £199.76

6. Yes; {strip > 197 cm}

7. *(a)*

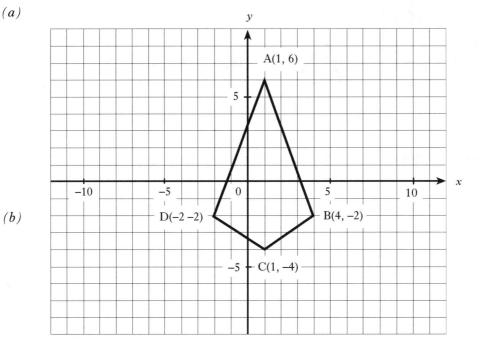

(b)

(c) Gradient of AB $= \dfrac{-8}{3}$

8. Area $\doteqdot$ 3190 cm^2

9. *(a)*

Number of posts (P)	1	2	3	4	▓	20
Number of chains (C)	0	2	4	6	▓	38

(b) $C = 2P - 2$ *(c)* 16 posts and 30 chains

10. *(a)* Scale drawing   Scale 1 cm: 1 km   *(b)* 255°

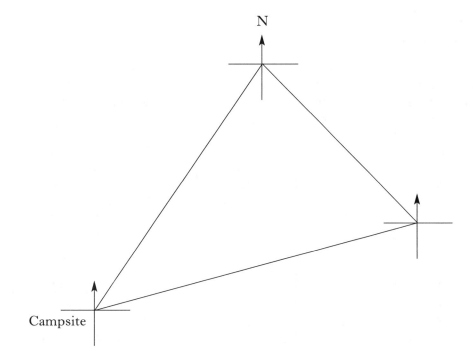

N

Campsite

11. £10 million

12. 4·51 m

13. 28 tins

14. *(a)* $x \geq \dfrac{19}{6}$ *(b)* $4(3ab - 2c)$

15.

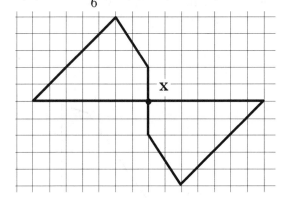

x

16. *(a)* $r = 10·4$ cm

  (b) No; {Since 3 diameters > 60 cm only 2 plates can be cut.}

17. £14.45

18. $V = 3016$ cm³

1.   *(a)* 8 °C   *(b)* 2 °C

2.   *(a)* £4   *(b)* 3·7%

3.

Number of teams getting 3 points	Number of teams getting 2 points	Number of teams getting 1 point	Number of teams getting 0 points	Total number of points
10	0	0	0	30
9	1	0	0	29
9	0	0	1	27
8	2	0	0	28
8	1	1	0	27
7	3	0	0	27

4.   *(a)* £108   *(b)* $\dfrac{11}{20}$

5.   *(a)* £45   *(b)* Greece

6. $y < 3$

7.   *(a)* 3 p.m.   *(b)* YES; 5.30 p.m. is earlier than 6 p.m.

8.

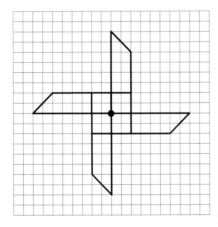

9.   *(a)* 56 miles   *(b)* £30.80
      (c) £2394.40
      (d)

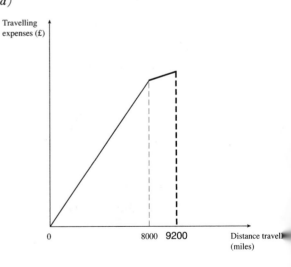

10.   *(a)*   Let the twins age = x years
            $3x + 3 = 42$
      (b)   Tamara is 16 years old

11.   *(a)* 34·6 cm   *(b)* 346 cm²

12.   *(a)* 20 cm   *(b)* 8·4 cm

13. $3(5w + 2st)$

14. *(a)* 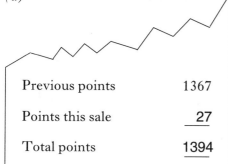 *(b)* £635

Previous points	1367
Points this sale	27
Total points	1394

15. *(a)* 1 *(b)*

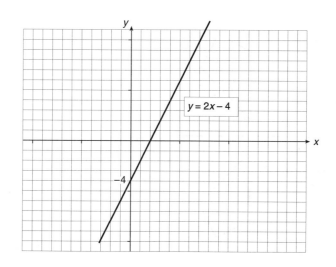

$y = 2x - 4$

−4

16. *(a)* 51·274 m
   (b) 52 m

17. *(a)*

Number of sections (s)	1	2	3	4		10
Number of girders (g)	3	7	11	15		39

(b) $g = 4s - 1$ *(c)* 419·15 m

18. 44

19. Yes; since $33·7° > 32°$

20. *(a)* $y = (x - 1)(x - 4)(x - 7)$ *(b)* $y = (x + 2)(x - 2)(x - 4)$

1999 — GENERAL MATHEMATICS ANSWERS

1. *(a)* £1   *(b)* 50p   *(c)* £7   **2.** £127.45

3. *(a)* 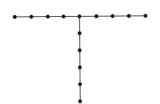   *(b)*

(s)	1	2	3	4	5		16
(d)	5	8	11	14	17		50

(c) $d = 3s + 2$ *(d)* $s = 33$

4. 90 calls

5.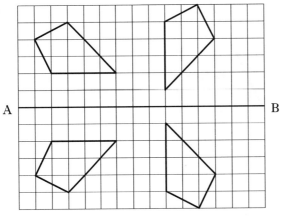

6. *(a)*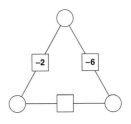

(b)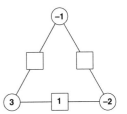

7. Mortgages Direct better by £198.40   **8.** $d \doteqdot 62 \cdot 5$ m

9. *(a)*

x	−3	0	3
y	−8	1	10

(b)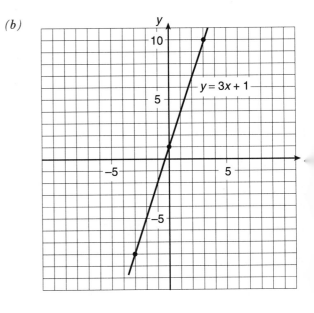

10.   *(a)* $\hat{BPO} = 22°$ *(b)* $x° = 46°$

11.   *(a)*   2010 cm   *(b)*   33·5 cm per s

12. $h \doteqdot 83·3$ m   **13.**   YES: {Since 28 m > 27·6 m}

14.   *(a)* $14a - 15$ *(b)* $x = \dfrac{8}{3}$

15.   *(a)*   *(b)*   Port Q, nearest port.   *(c)*   Bearing 232°, distance 32 km

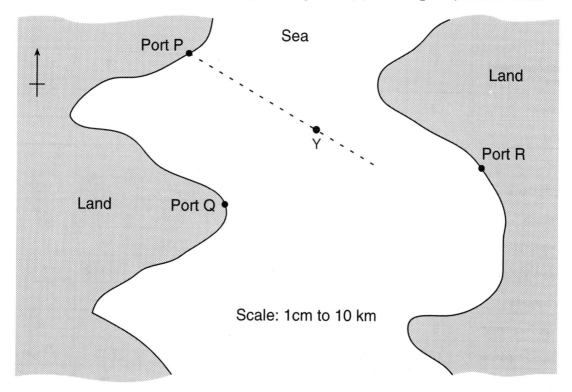

Sea

Port P

Land

Port R

Land   Port Q

Scale: 1cm to 10 km

16.   3·75 m   **17.**   *(a)*   36 discs   *(b)*   Area $\doteqdot 1482·6$ cm^2

18.   d = 18 km   **19.**   Vol = 11 250 000 mm^3

FREQUENCY CHART FOR GENERAL PAPERS

TOPICS	1993 Paper	1994 Paper	1995 Paper	1996 Paper	1997 Paper	1998 Paper	1999 Paper
NUMBER							
Calculations	3,16	6	2,4,17	3,5,15	2	1,3,14	
Approximation			12(b)				16
Index Notation	2			2	1		
Ratio			3			18	
Distance Speed, Time		12		8(c)		9	11(b)
Money	1,5	1	1,7	1.11	3(a),5	2,4,5	2,7
Time			5	6	3(b)	7	
SHAPE							
Scale Drawing	4	15	8	9	10		15
Similarity							13
Co-ordinates		9		4	7(a)(c)	15	
Area & Volume	11,17	3,10	12,15	7,18	8,16	11(b),12	17.19
Pythagoras	15	7	14	19(a)	6	11(a)	8
Angle Properties	6		16	13			10
Shape Properties	14	16,19	6	12	7(b),15	8,16	5,11(a)
Trigonometry	8	11	10	16	12	19	12
RELATIONSHIPS							
Patterns			9	10	4,9(a),13	17	3
Brackets				17(a)			14(a)
Factorisation			13		14(b)	13	
Formulae		8,17		19(b)	9(b)(c),18		6
Variation	13	18			17		4,18
Graphs & Tables	7,9,12	2,4,5,13		8,14	11	9(d),20	1,9
Equations	10		11	17(b)		10	14(b)
Inequations		14			14(a)	6	

Printed by Bell & Bain Ltd., Glasgow.